BEDTIME
Mindfulness

Written & Illustrated
by
Catherine Maven, M.A, OCELT

ISBN: 978-1-990333-07-1

Otter-Girl Press
Burlington, Ontario, Canada:

https://sleepingcat.wixsite.com/ottergirlpress

This book is dedicated to all of the loving and gifted teachers who taught me to be mindful and who expanded my awareness through their insights and practices.

These are questions for adults and children to consider daily at bedtime.

Be sure to take slow, calming breaths, which will help you sleep.

(Don't worry if you both fall asleep before you finish!)

First, close your eyes. Slowly take a deep breath, in through your nose and out through your mouth.
Picture the color RED and relax, relax, relax. Red is the color of energy and health.

What was the most fun thing you did today?

What part of your body enjoyed it the most? Was it your fingers or toes? Was it your legs or your tongue?

Picture the color

RED,

and relax.

Think about a worry or something that made you feel bad today. (You can say it out loud or just think it.)

Where is that feeling in your body? In your stomach, or another place?

Now imagine putting that bad feeling
in a balloon, and watch it lift up, up,
UP into the sky.

Bye-bye!

Picture the color

ORANGE,

and *relax.*

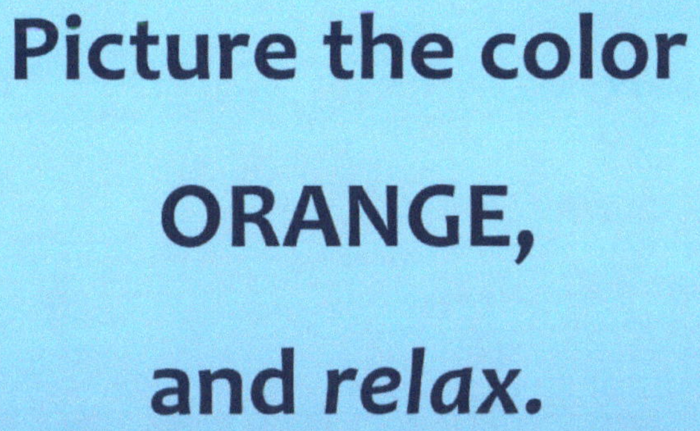

Slowly take another deep breath.
Your body is starting to feel warm and
heavy in your bed.
Picture the color YELLOW and relax,
relax, relax. Yellow is the color of
thoughts.

What did you dream about today?
Is there a happy thought you can
remember?

(You can say it out loud or just think it.)

Take that happy thought and plant it in
your heart like a seed.

Water it with love, and watch it
grow tall, like a yellow
sunflower.

Picture the color
YELLOW,
and *relax.*

Take a deep breath, in through your
nose and out through your mouth.

Picture the color GREEN and relax,
relax, relax.

Green is the color of nature.

Did you go out in nature today?

What did you see?

Can you remember one special

thing?

What was it?

Let green fill your heart and mind.

Nature is our friend
and brings us
joy!

Picture the color
GREEN,
and relax.

Take another deep breath.

Picture the color BLUE and relax,

relax, relax.

Blue is the color of peace.

Did you see a beautiful blue sky today?

Or blue water?

What blue thing did you see today?

If you were angry at someone today,
you can offer them peace in your
heart, right now.
You can forgive them.

Picture the color
BLUE,
and *relax.*

Take a deep breath.

Picture the color PURPLE and relax,

relax, relax.

Purple is the color of connection.

Who is your heart connected to?

Who makes your heart warm and happy?

(You can say it out loud or just think it.)

Imagine holding that person's hand,
and how good it feels.

Feel how that connection makes you
feel safe.

Picture the color
PURPLE,
and *relax.*

Take a deep breath. Picture the color
indigo and relax, relax, relax.

INDIGO is the color of your best self.

What did you do today that came
from your best self?

Did you help someone, or say
something kind?
What was it?

Helping others and being kind
builds our best self.
Our best self is connected to the best
self of everyone in the world.

Can you feel that, right now?

Picture the color

INDIGO,

and *relax*.

Let's repeat one more time:

Red, *relax.*

Orange, *relax.*

Yellow, *relax.*

Green, *relax.*

Blue, *relax.*

Purple, *relax.*

Indigo, *relax.*

Sweet
Dreams!

A Bit About Me:

I wrote my first short story when I was seven years old. While in university, I wrote a weekly humor column for the *McMaster Silhouette* newspaper, won some prizes for my writing, and was invited to publish a bit of my poetry.

Later, I scored a job as the Regional Reporter for a group of weekly newspapers in Hamilton, Ontario, Canada. These days, I teach English to immigrants. I have self-published a number of books on Amazon,

I'm also a visual artist who sells paintings and upcycled home décor items. I have just started illustrating my own books, using a digital watercolor collage technique.

Since most of my stories and paintings come to me in dreams, I never really know WHAT I'll do next. Regardless of the genre, though, I want my work to encourage people to embrace diversity.

Thanks for reading!
- **Catherine**

https://www.catherinemaven.com/

@CatherineMavenArt

Catherine Maven
Writings & Poetry